piano • vocal • guitar

# Poodle Skirts & Ducktails

## 56 REAL GONE SONGS FROM THE BIRTH OF ROCK 'N' ROLL

D1085793

ISBN 0-7935-5898-0

HAL•LEONARD®
CORPORATION
7777 W. BLUEMOUND RD. P.O. BOX 13819 MILWAUKEE, WI 53213

piano • vocal • guitar

# Poodle Skirts & Ducktails

## CONTENTS

**24 All I Have to Do Is Dream**
The Everly Brothers, 1958

**30 All Shook Up**
Elvis Presley, 1957

**27 At the Hop**
Danny & The Juniors, 1957

**34 The Big Hurt**
Miss Toni Fisher, 1959

**39 Blue Suede Shoes**
Carl Perkins, 1956

**42 Blueberry Hill**
Fats Domino, 1957

**48 Book of Love**
The Monotones, 1958

**52 Bye Bye Love**
The Everly Brothers, 1957

**45 Charlie Brown**
The Coasters, 1959

**54 Dance with Me Henry
(The Wallflower)**
Georgia Gibbs, 1955

**60 Don't Be Cruel
(To a Heart That's True)**
Elvis Presley, 1956

**68 Enchanted**
The Platters, 1959

**72 Endlessly**
Brook Benton, 1959

**65 (Now and Then There's)
A Fool Such as I**
Elvis Presley, 1959

**78 Great Balls of Fire**
Jerry Lee Lewis, 1958

**81 Happy, Happy Birthday Baby**
The Tune Weavers, 1957

**86 Have I Told You Lately
That I Love You**
Ricky Nelson, 1957

**88 Heartbreak Hotel**
Elvis Presley, 1956

**92 Honest I Do**
Jimmy Reed, 1957

**95 Honeycomb**
Jimmie Rodgers, 1957

**98 I Want You, I Need You,
I Love You**
Elvis Presley, 1956

**100 Keep A-Knockin'**
Little Richard, 1957

**103 Ko Ko Mo (I Love You So)**
The Crew Cuts, 1955

**106 Little Darlin'**
The Diamonds, 1957

**109 Lollipop**
The Chordettes, 1958

**112 Long Tall Sally**
Little Richard, 1956

**118 Love Me Tender**
Elvis Presley, 1956

**115 (You've Got) The Magic Touch**
The Platters, 1956

**120 Maybe Baby**
The Crickets, 1958

**126 My Prayer**
The Platters, 1956

**123 Oh Boy!**
The Crickets, 1958

**130 Oh! Carol**
Neil Sedaka, 1959

**138 Peggy Sue**
Buddy Holly, 1957

**142 Primrose Lane**
Jerry Wallace, 1959

**133 Rock and Roll Is Here to Stay**
Danny & The Juniors, 1958

**144 Rock Around the Clock**
Bill Haley & His Comets, 1955

**146 Searchin'**
The Coasters, 1957

**150 See You Later, Alligator**
Bill Haley & His Comets, 1956

**158 77 Sunset Strip**
Don Ralke, 1959

**153 Shake, Rattle and Roll**
Bill Haley & His Comets, 1955

**162 Silhouettes**
The Rays, 1957

**166 Sixteen Candles**
The Crests, 1959

**168 Smoke Gets in Your Eyes**
The Platters, 1958

**170 Splish Splash**
Bobby Darin, 1958

**176 The Stroll**
The Diamonds, 1958

**180 Tammy**
Debbie Reynolds, 1957

**173 (Let Me Be Your) Teddy Bear**
Elvis Presley, 1957

**182 Tequila**
The Champs, 1958

**188 That'll Be the Day**
The Crickets, 1957

**185 Think It Over**
The Crickets, 1958

**190 Tutti Frutti**
Little Richard, 1956

**194 Venus**
Frankie Avalon, 1959

**198 Wake Up Little Susie**
The Everly Brothers, 1957

**201 The Walk**
Jimmy McCracklin, 1958

**204 Waterloo**
Stonewall Jackson, 1959

**206 Yakety Yak**
The Coasters, 1958

# THE ROCK 'N' ROLL REVOLUTION BEGINS

by Elaine Schmidt

In the eyes of the American public, rock 'n' roll was born in July, 1955 when Bill Haley and His Comets soared to the top of pop music charts with the now classic tune "Rock Around the Clock." At the time however, the group's rough sound and the bumptious style of rock 'n' roll music were anything but classic. While teenagers saw the music as exciting, rebellious and new, parents saw it as dangerous, foreign, threatening, and out of control. Some even considered it the work of the devil. For promoters it was a golden, money-making possibility, and to the rhythm & blues artists from whom much of the new music had been copied, it was yet another infuriating, white rip-off of a traditionally black musical form. Regardless of perspective, it was clear that something was happening that could not be ignored. Rock 'n' roll had been simmering for years on low power radio stations and small record labels, in the form of rhythm & blues, country & western, and various hybrids of the two. The explosion of rock 'n' roll into mainstream popular culture in 1955 and 1956 was the result of a complicated series of events and cultural shifts that allowed American teens and this raucous new music to latch on to one another. Once that bond was formed, no amount of parental protestation could shake it. Rock 'n' roll had arrived and was not going to go away.

As Americans look back to the fifties, nostalgia and shallow television and film recreations of the times distort the decade into a complacent, trouble-free, almost mindless era — poodle skirts, ducktails, saddle shoes, the '57 Chevy, Howdy Doody, coonskin caps, hula hoops, and three-D movies. Often forgotten are the realities of McCarthy's witch hunt for communists, loyalty oaths, blacklisting, the Korean War, Sputnik, atomic fears and backyard bomb shelters. On the one hand, Ike and Mamie Eisenhower presided over the country like a favorite aunt and uncle, and Lucille Ball reigned as queen of television. On the other hand, Americans were testing atomic bombs at Bikini, teenage gangs were running rampant in larger cities, and public schools were under constant condemnation for failing to educate youth. Many teenagers had a dim view of their elders. As Freud's ideas from early in the century became the pop psychology of the 1950s, teens felt adults were to blame for every bad thing that happened. The stage was set for rebellion.

## "Race Music"

Another social factor in the rock 'n' roll revolution came from America's failed relationship with its black citizens. When civil rights legislation was passed by the Federal government in the late fifties, it was the first significant progress in that area since post-Civil War reconstruction. In many states African-Americans could not

4

dine, work, study or even ride the bus with whites. "Race music," which became known as rhythm & blues in 1949 thanks to *Billboard* magazine, was the music of urban black culture. A combination of traditional African rhythms, Gospel fervor, slave songs of work and struggle, as well as influence from the more modern jazz evolved the compelling, unique form of rhythm & blues. To many white Americans of the fifties, particularly teens, R & B music was wildly exotic and fascinating. African-American musicians were largely excluded from the mainstream of the popular music world. If a rhythm & blues record became popular, a white group was quickly hired to do a "cover" recording of the song. The cover would then be promoted to mainstream radio stations and record stores. In 1954, for instance, a rhythm & blues group known as the Chords recorded the song "Sh-Boom" for the Cat label. A white group called the Crew Cuts recorded the cover version that same year and both versions went to the top of their respective charts, but the white cover, which had far more airplay, reached a wider market and made much, much more money.

Fats (Antoine) Domino played with a merry, effortless style despite severe injuries to his hands during his youth.

As the music industry busily pigeon-holed and segregated music, the listening public began to disregard the divisions, purchasing and listening to what they liked. In Cleveland a disc jockey named Alan Freed was approached by one Leo Mintz, owner of a local record store, who reported that whites were buying rhythm & blues records in large numbers. It was 1951 and Freed, who was then playing all classical music on the air, tried playing a little rhythm & blues after his classical programming. Soon overwhelmed with requests for more R & B, he dropped classical music entirely. Choosing the tune "Blues for Moon Dog" as his theme song, and changing the name of his show from "Record Rendezvous" to "The Moon Dog Rock 'n' Roll House Party," Freed effectively coined the term "rock 'n' roll." In reality, Freed lifted the term from rhythm & blues music where "rocking and rolling" had long been a euphemism for sex. He went on to pioneer the rapid-fire, stylized patter that became standard fare among rock 'n' roll DJs.

◀ The Ducktail.

Freed began staging live concerts by rhythm & blues/rock 'n' roll musicians. 18,000 tickets were sold for a Freed-sponsored concert at the 10,000 seat Cleveland arena on March 21, 1952. The ensuing riots did not upset the establishment nearly as much as the fact that the crowd was half black and half white. Freed was accused of mixing races and was badgered by segregationalists who thought he should play white "covers" as opposed to black originals. Despite the flak, Freed continued to hold nonsegregated concerts and dances. He is remembered for his claims of naming rock 'n' roll, but more importantly for staging the over-sold Cleveland arena concert on the date purists call "the birthday of rock 'n' roll." Freed was not destined to remain a pivotal figure in the new musical style.

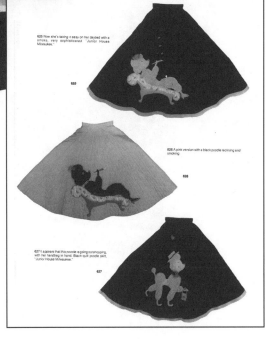

◀ Poodle Skirts.

By the end of the decade his career would be destroyed in a scandal involving his acceptance of "payola" from record companies in exchange for giving certain records more air-play than others. While the practice had gone on for years, Freed was made a scapegoat of sorts for industry-wide corruption.

## The Roots of Rock

America had been through a wringer during the 1930s and 1940s. The stock market crash of 1929 began an era of shocking poverty throughout much of the country. The pivotal event in ending the economic malaise was involvement in World War II. After the war, returning soldiers scrambled to find housing and jobs as they started families and tried to recapture the years lost in uniform. The first audience for rock 'n' roll was not made up of the much-heralded baby boomers born in the aftermath of World War II. It was made up of a slightly earlier generation — the first batch of American teenagers in many years to be raised without the looming specters of world war or poverty. They were lighthearted at an age when their parents had been burdened by a host of adult concerns. It was 1948 when the term "teenager" was first coined. Marketers quickly jumped on teenagers as a new demographic target group, realizing that the post-war affluence of adults was having a trickle-down effect to their children.

Whether coincidentally or not, 1948 was also the year that recording technology took strides forward. It was the year in which Columbia introduced the high-fidelity, micro-groove, long-playing record. Known as LPs, the 12 inch, vinyl records played at a speed of 33 and 1/3 rpm (revolutions per minute). RCA Victor countered six months later with the seven-inch single, also unbreakable, offering one song per side. Selling at under one dollar per single, and playable on phonographs that could be purchased for as little as $12.95, the single record was an instant hit among the newly targeted teenagers. But the innovation that made rock 'n' roll a constant companion to teens was the inexpensive, battery operated radio. Introduced a few years later, in 1954, the small, easily portable radios allowed teenagers constant access to their music of choice with freedom from parental censorship. From their first appearance, the small radios sold at a pace of some 10 million per year.

Television too, while still in its infancy, helped set the stage for rock 'n' roll. During the late forties, televisions quickly became fixtures in American homes, replacing the radio just as the radio had replaced the parlor piano some years earlier. Radio listenership dropped steadily and radio stations, unable to compete with the dynamic video aspect of television news and entertainment, switched to all-music

formats. In addition, many stations adopted a specialty genre. Some stations played all classical music, others all mainstream pop, country & western, rhythm & blues or jazz. They attempted to cultivate loyal followers of a specific audience.

# The Birth of BMI

The on-going turmoil of the music industry also contributed to the appearance of rock 'n' roll. The American Society of Composers, Authors and Publishers (ASCAP), had held the rights to most popular music since its organization in 1914. During the late 1930s sheet music sales took a downturn as recordings and radio gradually increased in popularity. ASCAP began to look to broadcasters for increased revenues. The ASCAP contracts with the National Association of Broadcasters, the American Federation of Musicians and the American Federation of Radio Artists, which dictated the royalty "rules" for air-play of popular music, all came due for renewal in 1940. Knowing that they were in for battle over the cost of playing music over on the air, broadcasters established Broadcast Music Incorporated (BMI) in 1939. When ASCAP presented new contracts to the broadcasters in March 1940, demanding a heavy percentage of stations' gross profits for the right to play ASCAP music, BMI immediately responded by securing performing rights to several significant catalogs of music, much of which was country, hillbilly and southern.

On January 1, 1941, the vast majority of broadcasters began a ten month ban on ASCAP music. Unfortunately for ASCAP, there was hardly a dent made in what went out over the airwaves. ASCAP had been dominating broadcasts with repeated plays of a small number of songs. ASCAP finally settled the contracts, taking far less in royalties than first demanded. Having broken the ASCAP monopoly, BMI continued handling performance rights for non-mainstream pop music. The result was a new prosperity for previously overlooked or excluded pop musicians. BMI also followed play lists around the country, not just in New York as was the ASCAP fashion, taking a national sampling of record popularity. In July 1942, the music industry apple-cart was again upset, this time with a recording ban instituted by the American Federation of Musicians. The musicians saw the increasing use of recordings on radio and juke boxes as a threat to employment for musicians. War-time restrictions on travel, and rationing of gas and tires increased the employment problem by making it difficult for dance bands to tour. Lobbying to establish a Musicians Unemployment Fund, the union began a two-year recording ban. The ban, which affected instrumentalists and not vocalists, resulted in a sudden rise in the popularity of vocal recordings that continued well into the next decade. Black jazz and rhythm & blues musicians who had been largely ignored by the union prior to the war, either released bootleg recordings or joined the union. Either choice led to their increased profits and popularity.

# Further Roots of Rock

World War II itself played an important part in the growth of rock 'n' roll. Prior to the war, most Americans lived fairly insular lives. Southerners had little reason to migrate to the north and Northerners little reason to go south. Many folks in the south listened to mostly gospel, jazz, rhythm & blues and some hillbilly music.

The popular Thunderbird, better known as the T-Bird.

When automobiles went back into production following World War II, Americans couldn't buy them fast enough. The new "car culture" led to suburban growth, family vacations and the appearance of the motel, or motor-hotel.

In the west, country music and western music, still two distinct elements, were the vogue among the common folk. To the north and east, it was predominantly Tin Pan Alley songs and Broadway show tunes that were heard. The "Hit Parade" songs were heard by most Americans. Beyond that, music was regionally centered. During the war, service men were forced to move to various corners of the country and found themselves living in close quarters with a wide variety of diverse Americans. Civilians too relocated, most for employment in war-related industries. The result was that western music turned up in the south as rhythm & blues appeared in New York and Chicago. Many Americans were exposed to different facets of American music for the first time. It was during the war years that rhythm & blues first came into demand in juke boxes throughout the country.

In 1952 the United States exploded the first hydrogen bomb. By November 1, 1958, over 300 test explosions would be detonated.

Teenagers, rebellious and recently identified as a viable demographic group, were equipped with affordable records and radios just as rhythm & blues and rock 'n' roll came to the attention of the American public. While their parents listened to Eddie Fisher, Rosemary Clooney, Frank Sinatra and Pat Boone accompanied by full orchestras, teens began to tune in to the new sounds of Chuck Berry, Bill Haley and Fats Domino accompanied by guitars, drums and saxophones. Adults initially responded with shock to the rough-edged sounds and frenetic movements of rock 'n' roll musicians. In some parts of the country rock 'n' roll was banned from the airwaves, and in the homes of many teenagers it was strictly forbidden. Sermons were delivered on the evils of rock 'n' roll while performers of traditional popular song publicly dismissed rock as a tacky, passing fad. Teens embraced rock 'n' roll as an integral part of their new identity, most of them oblivious to the sexual basis of some the lyrics. "Their" music was nothing like the "Tennessee Waltz" to which their parents listened. However outraged parents were, teens could not be stopped from listening to it and buying it.

# The Movies and Early Rock Stars

Rock 'n' roll was quickly wedded to youthful rebellion in movies like *Blackboard Jungle* of 1955. The film, which carried a message about the decay of American schools, featured Bill Haley's song "Rock Around the Clock." Stunned by the success of *Blackboard Jungle*, and quick to realize the potential of rock in films, producer Sam Katzman quickly put Bill Haley on screen, along with popular D.J. Alan Freed and The Platters, in the late-1955 film *Rock Around the Clock*. With the Platters singing "Only You" and "The Great Pretender" and Haley and His Comets belting out hits like "Rock Around the Clock" and "See You Later Alligator," the bland plot of the movie had little to do with its success. The only thing more amazing than the response of American teens to *Rock Around the Clock* was the response of British and other European teens to it. Riots broke out nearly everywhere the film played, putting Haley and the new rock 'n' roll music into international headlines. Teens immediately lined up to see the host of *Rock Around the Clock* rip-offs that followed.

Actor James Dean was the quintessential restless, fifties teen. After making only three feature films he became a cult hero after his 1955 death in a car crash.

WELCOME BACK! ELVIS PRESLEY YOU'RE THE GREATEST!

METRO-GOLDWYN-MAYER presents

**Jailhouse Rock**

in CinemaScope · An Avon Production

Judy Tyler · Mickey Shaughnessy · Dean Jones · Jennifer Holden · Guy Trosper

Richard Thorpe · Pandro S. Berman

Rock 'n' roll had dug in its heels by the end of 1955. The next few years would see the rise and fall of dozens of rhythm & blues-based artists, their industry-created cover groups and many original acts as well. Buddy Holly, singing with his trademark hiccup and wearing conservative suits and dark-rimmed glasses, would have a huge impact on rock 'n' roll before his death in 1959. Ground-breaking Bill Haley would only last a few years as a Rock and Roll star, largely relegated to revivals of early rock 'n' roll after about 1957. Frankie Avalon, whose 1959 "Venus" was a huge success, was a carefully marketed teen idol. His boyish good looks and clean-cut image made him palatable to adults and "dreamy" to teen girls. Little Richard was best known for his 1956 hit "Tutti Frutti," and two hits from 1957, "Keep a Knockin" and "Good Golly Miss Molly." He disappeared from the still-new rock scene in 1957 to become a preacher who then denounced the evils of rock 'n' roll.

Jerry Lee Lewis, known for his 1958 hit "Great Balls of Fire," was effectively shunned from the business after his 1958 marriage to a 13 year-old cousin. Teen idol Ricky Nelson began his career in radio as a child, found rock 'n' roll teen-idol status with "Have I Told You Lately That I Love You" in 1957, and later moved on to country music.

▶ With his knees bent and feet splayed, the suggestive dance of Elvis' early performances quickly became his signature.

## Elvis

And then there was Elvis. Born in Tupelo, Mississippi, in 1935, Elvis Presley walked into a Memphis recording studio one day to cut a record as a birthday gift for his mother. Sam Phillips of the Sun label took one look at Presley and knew he had struck gold. Elvis was a white musician with a black sound, whose roots in rhythm & blues, gospel and country gave him a genuinely unique style. Presley was moody and rebellious, both pluses in appealing to the teen-aged set. When his 1954 "That's All Right Mama" was first aired, DJs and audiences alike assumed that the southern singer was black. Elvis's early hits, including 1956 "Don't Be Cruel" and "Love Me Tender," were eclipsed by the furor his stage presence created. After Elvis performed in Oakland, California, a police officer commented on the singer's now famous gyrations saying, "If he did that in the street, we'd arrest him." Seeing the uproar that followed his first television appearances, on the 1956 Dorsey Brothers "Stage Show" and on "The Milton Berle Show," television producers were fearful of presenting him. Steve Allen put him on the air, but dressed him in a tuxedo and made him sing "Hound Dog" to a real dog. When Ed Sullivan finally broke down and introduced him, it was with the stipulation that he would be filmed only from the waist up. Jokingly called "Elvis the Pelvis" in his early years, Elvis went on to reign as the "King of Rock 'n' Roll" or simply "The King." He entered the army in 1958, a move calculated to change his dubious image. After his return from the service in 1960 he was a changed man. He had served his country with no special treatment, thus gaining adult approval. The subsequent move to films was part of a carefully orchestrated move toward respectability. To this day his early recordings on the Sun label are considered by many to be his finest.

As the fifties progressed, rock 'n' roll records made up an ever increasing share of the *Billboard* music charts. Rock 'n' roll had proved itself. It was not a passing fad, but it was a changing entity. Rock 'n' roll would change shape and focus at a breathtaking pace over the coming years, making political and social commentaries and expanding to reach an ever broader audience. Somehow the hits of rock 'n' roll's early years would never die away. The early classics of have remained a part of the musical vocabulary of not just the people who discovered the music as teens during the fifties, but of the whole world. Rock 'n' roll, it would seem, really is here to stay.

▲
"Juvenile delinquents"

▲
Bill Haley and His Comets, the group that first brought rock 'n' roll to a wide audience of American teens.

# AMERICA IN
# 1954

The stylish Corvette first appeared in 1954.
▼

## MOST POPULAR
## TV SHOWS:

I Love Lucy
The Jackie Gleason Show
Dragnet
You Bet Your Life
The Toast of the Town
Disneyland
The Jack Benny Show
The Martha Raye Show
The George Gobel Show
Ford Theatre

## ACADEMY AWARDS:

Best Picture:      *On the Waterfront*
Best Director:     Elia Kazan
                   *(On the Waterfront)*
Best Actress:      Grace Kelly
                   *(The Country Girl)*
Best Actor:        Marlon Brando
                   *(On the Waterfront)*

## OTHER POPULAR FILMS:

*The Caine Mutiny*
*Seven Brides for Seven Brothers*
*Three Coins in the Fountain*
*Rear Window*
*A Star Is Born*
*Dial M for Murder*

## THE YEAR'S TOP TEN SONGS:

1. Oh! My Pa-Pa
   *Eddie Fisher*
2. Secret Love
   *Doris Day*
3. Make Love to Me!
   *Jo Stafford*
4. Wanted
   *Perry Como*
5. Little Things Mean a Lot
   *Kitty Kallen*
6. Three Coins in the Fountain
   *Four Aces*
7. Sh-Boom
   *The Crew-Cuts*
8. Hey There
   *Rosemary Clooney*
9. This Ole House
   *Rosemary Clooney*
10. I Need You Now
    *Eddie Fisher*

▲
Ike, Dwight David Eisenhower, was U.S. President from 1952-1960. "The great problem of America today," he said in 1952, "is to take that straight road down the middle."

▲
[Top] "The Honeymooners," starring Jackie Gleason, Art Carney, Audrey Meadows and Joyce Randolph, debuted in 1955.

[Bottom] The decade's reigning queen of comedy, Lucille Ball, delivered ridiculous stunts, far-fetched situations and outrageous antics. "I Love Lucy" premiered in 1951, landing in the year-end Nielsen Top Ten ratings for six consecutive years.

# AMERICA IN 1954

## BEST SELLING BOOKS:

*Mary Anne*, Daphne Du Maurier

*Love Is Eternal*, Irving Stone

*Sweet Thursday*, John Steinbeck

*Never Victorious, Never Defeated*, Taylor Caldwell

*The Holy Bible: Revised Standard Version*

*The Power of Positive Thinking*, Norman Vincent Peale

*Better Homes and Gardens New Cook Book*

*Betty Crocker's Good and Easy Cook Book*

## OPENING ON BROADWAY:

*The Bad Seed*
*Witness for the Prosecution*
*The Rainmaker*
*The Pajama Game*
*The Boy Friend*
*Peter Pan*
*The Threepenny Opera*

## WORLD SERIES WINNER:

New York beats Cleveland 4 to 0

## HEROES:

Mildred "Babe" Didrikson Zaharias wins the U.S. Women's Open golf tournament.

"Lassie" wins an Emmy.

Jonas Salk begins to innoculate schoolchildren against the dreaded, crippling disease polio. In a few years the disease is vanquished.

Joseph Welch becomes the hero of the televised Army-McCarthy hearings in which the crusading Joseph McCarthy loses popular support.

Wladzui Valentino Liberace becomes a TV star. While critics assail his piano playing, audiences love his flamboyant style and sparkling grin.

## FADS:

Felt circle-skirts with poodle appliques
Panty raids
Ducktail hairstyles
Roller skating marathons

# AMERICA IN 1955

## MOST POPULAR TV SHOWS:

*The $64,000 Question*
*I Love Lucy*
*The Ed Sullivan Show*
*Disneyland*
*The Jack Benny Show*
*December Bride*
*You Bet Your Life*
*Dragnet*
*The Millionaire*
*I've Got a Secret*

## ACADEMY AWARDS:

Best Picture:     *Marty*
Best Director:   Delbert Mann (*Marty*)
Best Actress:    Anna Magnani (*The Rose Tattoo*)
Best Actor:      Ernest Borgnine (*Marty*)

## OTHER POPULAR FILMS:

*Rebel Without a Cause*
*The Blackboard Jungle*
*Mister Roberts*
*Love Is a Many Splendored Thing*
*The Man with the Golden Arm*
*The Bridges at Toko-Ri*
*Oklahoma!*

## THE YEAR'S TOP TEN SONGS:

1. Rock Around the Clock
   *Bill Haley & His Comets*
2. Sixteen Tons
   *Tennessee Ernie Ford*
3. Love Is a Many Splendored Thing
   *Four Aces*
4. The Yellow Rose of Texas
   *Mitch Miller*
5. Autumn Leaves
   *Roger Williams*
6. Learnin' the Blues
   *Frank Sinatra*
7. Ain't That a Shame
   *Pat Boone*
8. Moments to Remember
   *The Four Lads*
9. I Hear You Knocking
   *Gale Storm*
10. A Blossom Fell
    *Nat "King" Cole*

"The $64,000 Question" premiered in 1955, part of a wave of popular TV quiz shows. (Library of Congress)
▼

◄ A scene from the gritty, message film *Blackboard Jungle.* The film featured the song "Rock Around the Clock" performed by Bill Haley and His Comets. (MGM)

▲
"Gunsmoke," the first
adult western on TV,
was first aired in 1955.

# AMERICA IN 1955

## BEST SELLING BOOKS:

*Margorie Morningstar*,
Herman Wouk

*Auntie Mame*,
Patrick Dennis

*The Man in the Gray Flannel Suit*,
Sloan Wilson

*The Tontine*,
Thomas B. Costain

*The Power of Positive Thinking*,
Norman Vincent Peale

*The Secret of Happiness*,
Billy Graham

*How to Live 365 Days a Year*,
John A. Schindler

*Why Johnny Can't Read*,
Rudolf Flesch

## OPENING ON BROADWAY:

*Cat on a Hot Tin Roof*
*The Matchmaker*
*Bus Stop*
*The Diary of Anne Frank*
*A View from the Bridge*
*Damn Yankees*
*Silk Stockings*

## WORLD SERIES WINNER:

Brooklyn beats New York, 4 to 3

## HEROES:

Actor James Dean takes on near cult status following his death in an automobile accident.

The Hiroshima Maidens, 25 young Japanese women badly scarred by the atomic bombs dropped on Japan, arrive in the United States for free reconstructive and plastic surgery.

## FADS:

Pizza
Ford Thunderbird
Mooning
Davy Crockett coonskin caps

▲
A scene from *Rebel Without a Cause*,
released in 1955, with James Dean
and Natalie Wood.(Warner Bros.)

# AMERICA IN 1956

## MOST POPULAR TV SHOWS:

*I Love Lucy*
*The Ed Sullivan Show*
*General Electric Theater*
*The $64,000 Question*
*December Bride*
*Alfred Hitchcock Presents*
*I've Got a Secret*
*Gunsmoke*
*The Perry Como Show*
*The Jack Benny Show*

## ACADEMY AWARDS:

Best Picture:
*Around the World in Eighty Days*

Best Director:
George Stevens (*Giant*)

Best Actress:
Ingrid Bergman (*Anastasia*)

Best Actor:
Yul Brynner (*The King and I*)

## OTHER POPULAR FILMS:

*War and Peace*
*Friendly Persuasion*
*The Ten Commandments*
*Love Me Tender*
*Bus Stop*
*Invasion of the Body Snatchers*
*The Seventh Seal*

## THE YEAR'S TOP TEN SONGS:

1. Don't Be Cruel/Hound Dog
   *Elvis Presley*
2. Singing the Blues
   *Guy Mitchell*
3. The Wayward Wind
   *Gogi Grant*
4. Heartbreak Hotel
   *Elvis Presley*
5. Rock and Roll Waltz
   *Kay Starr*
6. The Poor People of Paris
   *Les Baxter*
7. Memories Are Made of This
   *Dean Martin*
8. Love Me Tender
   *Elvis Presley*
9. My Prayer
   *The Platters*
10. Lisbon Antigua
    *Nelson Riddle*

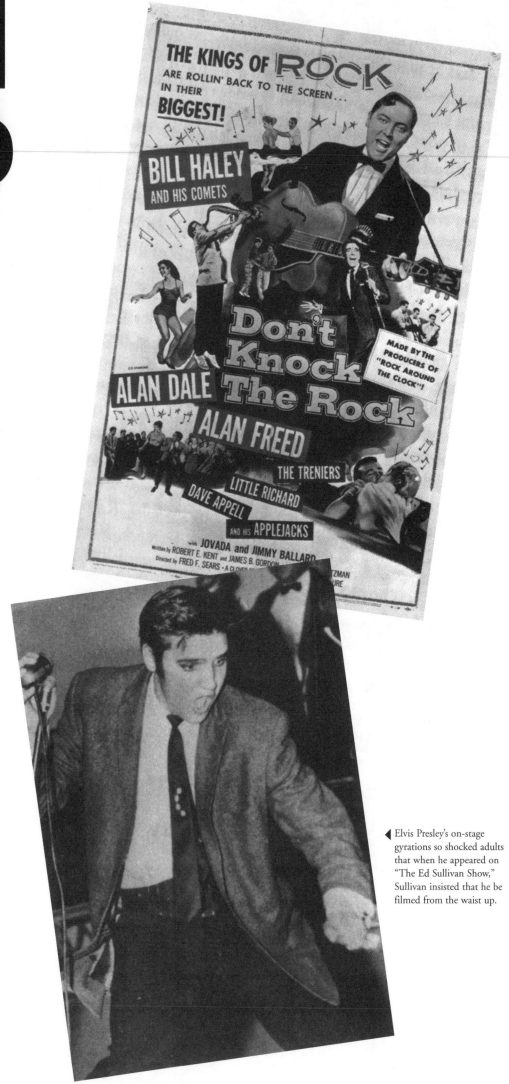

◄ Elvis Presley's on-stage gyrations so shocked adults that when he appeared on "The Ed Sullivan Show," Sullivan insisted that he be filmed from the waist up.

# AMERICA IN 1956

Lines began forming at 4:00 AM for tickets to the Broadway production of *My Fair Lady*, starring Rex Harrison and Julie Andrews.

A scene from *My Fair Lady* on Broadway, with Robert Coote, Julie Andrews and Rex Harrison.

## BEST SELLING BOOKS:

*The Last Hurrah*,
Edwin O'Connor

*Peyton Place*,
Grace Metalious

*Auntie Mame*,
Patrick Dennis

*Betty Crocker's Picture Cook Book Etiquette*,
Francis Benton

*The Nun's Story*,
Kathryn Hulme

## OPENING ON BROADWAY:

*Waiting for Godot*
*Long Day's Journey into Night*
*Auntie Mame*
*My Fair Lady*
*The Most Happy Fella*
*Li'l Abner*
*Candide*

## WORLD SERIES WINNER:

New York beats Brooklyn 4 to 3

## HEROES:

Opera singer Maria Callas make her Metropolitan Opera debut, setting a box office record for opening night revenues.

Movie stars include John Wayne, James Stewart, Gary Cooper and Marilyn Monroe.

Beverly Sills makes her operatic debut in Central City, Colorado with *The Ballad of Baby Doe*.

## FADS:

Circular buildings
Seventeen recordings of the Ballad of Davy Crockett on the market
Television more popular than films
Drive-in theaters
"As the World Turns" and "The Edge of Night" air

# AMERICA IN 1957

Charles Van Doren appears to struggle with a question during filming of the quiz show "Twenty-One." Van Doren later admitted that he had been given answers. The story was the subject of the 1994 film *Quiz Show*.

## MOST POPULAR TV SHOWS:

*Gunsmoke*
*The Danny Thomas Show*
*Tales of Wells Fargo*
*Have Gun, Will Travel*
*I've Got a Secret*
*The Life and Legend of Wyatt Earp*
*General Electric Theater*
*The Restless Gun*
*December Bride*
*You Bet Your Life*

## ACADEMY AWARDS:

Best Picture:   *The Bridge on the River Kwai*
Best Director: David Lean
        (*The Bridge on the River Kwai*)
Best Actress:   Joanne Woodward
        (*The Three Faces of Eve*)
Best Actor:     Alec Guinness
        (*The Bridge on the River Kwai*)

## OTHER POPULAR FILMS:

*Peyton Place*
*Sayonara*
*Twelve Angry Men*
*Witness for the Prosecution*
*The Prince and the Showgirl*
*Silk Stockings*
*Love in the Afternoon*
*Les Girls*

## THE YEAR'S TOP TEN SONGS:

1.   All Shook Up
     *Elvis Presley*
2.   Love Letters in the Sand
     *Pat Boone*
3.   Jailhouse Rock
     *Elvis Presley*
4.   (Let Me Be Your) Teddy Bear
     *Elvis Presley*
5.   April Love
     *Pat Boone*
6.   Young Love
     *Tab Hunter*
7.   Tammy
     *Debbie Reynolds*
8.   Honeycomb
     *Jimmie Rodgers*
9.   Wake Up Little Susie
     *The Everly Brothers*
10.  You Send Me
     *Sam Cooke*

WELCOME BACK! ELVIS PRESLEY YOU'RE THE GREATEST!

METRO-GOLDWYN-MAYER presents

Jailhouse Rock

in CinemaScope · An Avon Production

Judy Tyler · Mickey Shaughnessy · Dean Jones · Jennifer Holden · Guy Trosper
Richard Thorpe · Pandro S. Berman

# AMERICA IN 1957

▲
Marilyn Monroe in *The Seven Year Itch*. (20th Century-Fox)

▲
Buddy Holly and the Crickets.

**BEST SELLING BOOKS:**

*By Love Possessed,*
James Gould Cozzens

*Peyton Place,*
Grace Metalious

*On the Beach,*
Nevil Shute

*Atlas Shrugged,*
Ayn Rand

*Kids Say the Darndest Things!,*
Art Linkletter

*Please Don't Eat the Daisies,*
Jean Kerr

*Better Homes and Gardens Flower Arranging*

**OPENING ON BROADWAY:**

*West Side Story*
*The Music Man*
*Ziegfeld Follies (the last Ziegfeld)*
*Look Homeward, Angel*
*The Dark at the Top of the Stairs*
*Romanoff and Juliet*
*A Moon for the Misbegotten*

**WORLD SERIES WINNER:**

Milwaukee beats New York 4 to 3

**HEROES:**

When Charles Van Doren wins $129,000 on the quiz show "Twenty-One", he is flooded with letters that hail him as a national hereo and the antithesis of Elvis Presley.

Dick Clark brings "American Bandstand" to the country.

The Everly Brothers' record "Wake Up Little Susie" is banned in Boston, which brings it huge sales throughout the country.

**FADS:**

Crinolines
The bunny hop
Hula hoops
Slinky
Silly Putty
Frisbees
Volkswagon Beetles

# AMERICA IN 1958

## MOST POPULAR TV SHOWS:

*Gunsmoke*
*Wagon Train*
*Have Gun, Will Travel*
*The Danny Thomas Show*
*Maverick*
*Tales of Wells Fargo*
*The Real McCoys*
*I've Got a Secret*
*The Life and Legend of Wyatt Earp*

## ACADEMY AWARDS:

Best Picture: *Gigi*
Best Director: Vincente Minnelli *(Gigi)*
Best Actress: Susan Hayward *(I Want to Live)*
Best Actor: David Niven *(Separate Tables)*

## OTHER POPULAR FILMS:

*Auntie Mame*
*Cat on a Hot Tin Roof*
*The Defiant Ones*
*The Inn of the Sixth Happiness*
*Some Came Running*
*South Pacific*
*Touch of Evil*
*Vertigo*

## THE YEAR'S TOP TEN SONGS:

1. At the Hop
   *Danny & The Juniors*
2. It's All in the Game
   *Tommy Edwards*
3. The Purple People Eater
   *Sheb Wooley*
4. All I Have to Do Is Dream
   *The Everly Brothers*
5. Tequila
   *The Champs*
6. Don't
   *Elvis Presley*
7. Nel Blu Dipinto Di Blu (Volare)
   *Domenico Modugno*
8. Sugartime
   *The McGuire Sisters*
9. He's Got the Whole World (In His Hands)
   *Laurie London*
10. The Chipmunk
    *The Chipmunks/David Seville*

"Atoms for Peace" postage stamp. During 1955 and 1958 conferences were held in Geneva that explored the atom's role in biology, medicine, agriculture and as a power source.

Clean-cut Frankie Avalon was deliberately groomed as a teen idol who would be acceptable to parents worried about the unseemly stars of rock 'n' roll. Pat Boone filled the same bill with parents.

Little Richard (Richard Wayne Penniman) epitomized the wild side of rock 'n' roll.

▼

## BEST SELLING BOOKS:

*Doctor Zhivago,*
Boris Pasternak

*Anatomy of a Murder,*
Robert Traver

*Lolita,*
Vladimir Nabokov

*Around the World with Auntie Mame,*
Patrick Dennis

*Ice Palace,*
Edna Ferber

*Kids Say the Darndest Things!,*
Art Linkletter

*Masters of Deceit,*
J. Edgar Hoover

*Better Homes and Gardens Salad Book*

*Inside Russia Today,*
John Gunther

*The New Testament in Modern English*

*Aku-Aku,*
Thor Heyerdahl

## OPENING ON BROADWAY:

*J.B.*
*The Marriage-Go-Round*
*The Visit*
*Ages of Man*
*The Entertainer*
*Flower Drum Song*
*La Plume de Ma Tante*

## WORLD SERIES WINNER:

New York beats Milwaukee 4 to 3

## HEROES:

Pianist Van Cliburn becomes the first American to win the Russian Tchaikovsky Competition. His youth and good looks win him uncommon popularity at home.

Eleanor Roosevelt is first on the list of Most Admired Women for the eleventh straight year. Queen Elizabeth comes in second.

Poet Jack Kerouac becomes the voice of the 'beat' generation.

## FADS:

Folk music
*Lolita*, in paperback, sells one million copies
waterskiing

◄ The first "earthlings" in space.

# AMERICA IN 1959

## MOST POPULAR TV SHOWS:

*Gunsmoke*
*Wagon Train*
*Have Gun, Will Travel*
*The Danny Thomas Show*
*The Red Skelton Show*
*Father Knows Best*
*77 Sunset Strip*
*The Price Is Right*
*Wanted: Dead or Alive*
*Perry Mason*

## ACADEMY AWARDS:

Best Picture:   *Ben-Hur*
Best Director:  William Wyler *(Ben-Hur)*
Best Actress:   Simone Signoret
                *(Room at the Top)*
Best Actor:     Charlton Heston *(Ben-Hur)*

## OTHER POPULAR FILMS:

*Anatomy of a Murder*
*The Nun's Story*
*Room at the Top*
*Some Like It Hot*
*Pillow Talk*
*Suddenly, Last Summer*

## THE YEAR'S TOP TEN SONGS:

1. Mack the Knife
   *Bobby Darin*
2. The Battle of New Orleans
   *Johnny Horton*
3. Venus
   *Frankie Avalon*
4. Stagger Lee
   *Lloyd Price*
5. The Three Bells
   *The Browns*
6. Lonely Boy
   *Paul Anka*
7. Come Softly to Me
   *Fleetwoods*
8. Smoke Gets in Your Eyes
   *The Platters*
9. Heartaches By the Number
   *Guy Mitchell*
10. Sleep Walk
   *Santo & Johnny*

▲
Built in complete secrecy, loaded with gadgets
and preceded by unprecedented fanfare, the
Ford Edsel was the worst flop in automotive
history. The oval grille reminded critics of
"a toilet seat" or "an Oldsmobile sucking
an egg." (Library of Congress)

▲
The appearance of
the commercial transport jet
made the fifties an unprecedented
decade of travel for many Americans.

# AMERICA IN 1959

Civil defense drills in
schools and bomb shelters
in back yards were part
of the American response
to the cold war.
(Library of Congress)

## BEST SELLING BOOKS:
*Exodus*,
Leon Uris

*Doctor Zhivago*,
Boris Pasternak

*Hawaii*,
James Michener

*Lady Chatterly's Lover*,
D.H. Lawrence

*The Ugly American*,
William J. Lederer, Eugene L. Burdick

*The Status Seekers*,
Vance Packard

*Act One*,
Moss Hart

*The General Foods Kitchens Cookbook*

*Elements of Style*,
William Strunk, Jr., E. B. White

## OPENING ON BROADWAY:
*A Raisin in the Sun*
*The Miracle Worker*
*A Majority of One*
*Mark Twain Tonight*
*The Sound of Music*
*Once Upon a Mattress*
*Gypsy*

## WORLD SERIES WINNER:
Los Angeles beats Chicago 4 to 2

## HEROES:
Buddy Holly, The Big Bopper and Ritchie Valens are
seen as rock and roll martyrs after their deaths in a plane
crash near Clear Lake, Iowa.

Charles Van Doren admits to receiving answers prior to
tapings of the popular quiz show "Twenty-One". NBC is
swamped with letters that protest his dismissal as an
announcer.

## FADS:
Western toys
Go-karts
Black leotards worn with sleeveless jumpers
Films with scents

Drive-in theaters attempted to lure TV viewing
American families back to the movies by
offering refreshments served at the car window,
baby-sitters, and portable bottle warmers.

# ALL I HAVE TO DO IS DREAM

By BOUDLEAUX BRYANT

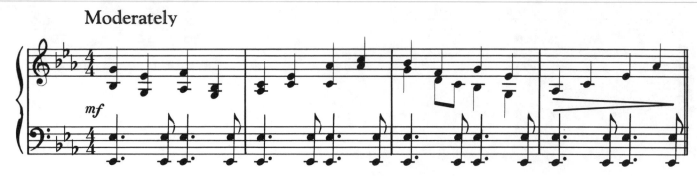

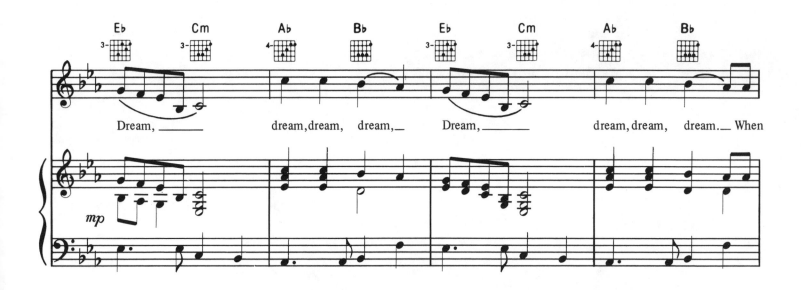

Dream, _____ dream, dream, dream, _ Dream, _____ dream, dream, dream._ When

I want you in my arms, When I want you and all your charms When
I feel blue in the night, And I need you to hold me tight When

# AT THE HOP

Words and Music by ARTHUR SINGER,
JOHN MADARA and DAVID WHITE

# ALL SHOOK UP

Words and Music by OTIS BLACKWELL
and ELVIS PRESLEY

# THE BIG HURT

Words and Music by
WAYNE SHANKLIN

# BLUE SUEDE SHOES

Words and Music by
CARL LEE PERKINS

Bright Tempo (not too fast)

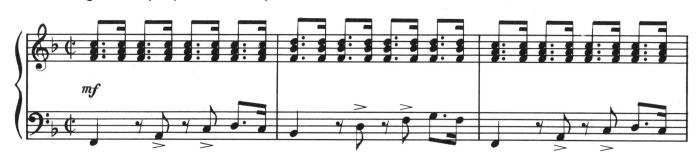

**Chorus**

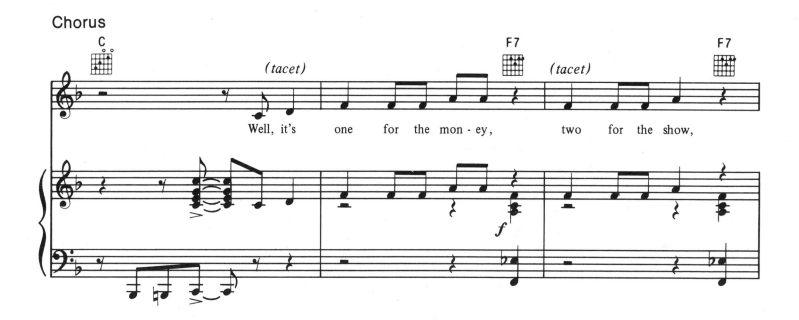

Well, it's one for the mon-ey, two for the show,

three to get read-y, now go, cat, go But don't you

# BLUEBERRY HILL

Words and Music by AL LEWIS,
LARRY STOCK and VINCENT ROSE

# CHARLIE BROWN

Words and Music by JERRY LEIBER
and MIKE STOLLER

# BOOK OF LOVE

Words and Music by WARREN DAVIS,
GEORGE MALONE and CHARLES PATRICK

# BYE BYE LOVE

Words and Music by FELICE BRYANT
and BOUDLEAUX BRYANT

Moderately fast

# DANCE WITH ME HENRY
## (THE WALLFLOWER)

Words and Music by HANK BALLARD,
ETTA JAMES and JOHNNY OTIS

56

# DON'T BE CRUEL
## (TO A HEART THAT'S TRUE)

Words and Music by OTIS BLACKWELL
and ELVIS PRESLEY

# (NOW AND THEN THERE'S)
# A FOOL SUCH AS I

Words and Music by
BILL TRADER

# ENCHANTED

Words and Music by
BUCK RAM

# ENDLESSLY

Words and Music by CLYDE OTIS
and BROOK BENTON

# GREAT BALLS OF FIRE

Words and Music by OTIS BLACKWELL
and JACK HAMMER

# HAPPY, HAPPY BIRTHDAY BABY

Words and Music by MARGO SYLVIA
and GILBERT LOPEZ

# HAVE I TOLD YOU LATELY THAT I LOVE YOU

Words and Music by
SCOTT WISEMAN

# HEARTBREAK HOTEL

Words and Music by MAE BOREN AXTON,
TOMMY DURDEN and ELVIS PRESLEY

I'll be so lone - ly _____ I could die. Al -

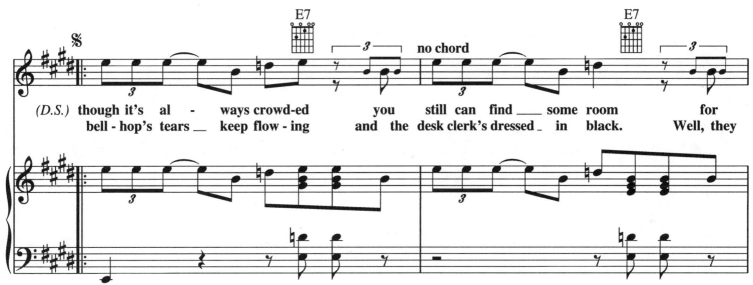

(D.S.) though it's al - ways crowd-ed      you    still can find ___ some room      for
bell - hop's tears _ keep flow - ing      and the desk clerk's dressed _ in black.      Well, they

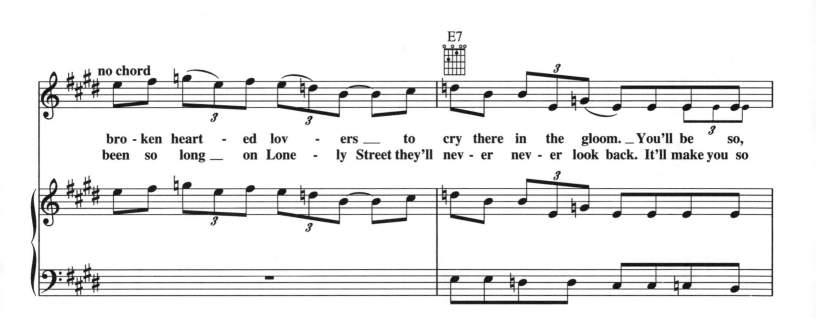

bro - ken heart - ed lov - ers ___ to   cry there in the gloom. _You'll be    so,
been so long _ on Lone - ly Street they'll nev - er nev - er look back. It'll make you so

# HONEST I DO

By JIMMY REED
and EWART G. ABNER, JR.

# HONEYCOMB

Words and Music by
BOB MERRILL

*Additional Lyrics*

2. Now have you heard tell how they made a bee?
   Then tried a hand at a green, green tree.
   So the tree was made and I guess you've heard,
   Next they made a bird.
   Then they went around lookin' everywhere,
   Takin' love from here and from there,
   And they stored it up in a little cart,
   For my honey's heart.
   *Chorus*

# I WANT YOU, I NEED YOU, I LOVE YOU

Words by MAURICE MYSELS
Music by IRA KOSLOFF

Moderately Slow

Hold me close, __ hold me tight; __ make me thrill __ with de-light. __ Let me know __ where I stand __ from the start. __ I Want You, I Need You, I Love You __ with all my heart. __ Ev-'ry time __ that you're near __ all my cares __ dis-ap-pear. __ Dar-ling,

# KEEP A-KNOCKIN'

Words and Music by
RICHARD PENNIMAN

Come back to-mor-row night and try it a - gain. ___

# KO KO MO
## (I LOVE YOU SO)

Words and Music by EUNICE LEVY,
JAKE PORTER and FOREST WILSON

# LITTLE DARLIN'

Words and Music by
MAURICE WILLIAMS

*(May be spoken over repeat:)*

**My dear, I need your love to call my own**
**And never do wrong; and to hold in mine your little hand.**
**I'll know too soon that I'll love again.**
**Please come back to me.**

# LOLLIPOP

Words and Music by BEVERLY ROSS
and JULIUS DIXON

# LONG TALL SALLY

Words and Music by ENOTRIS JOHNSON,
RICHARD PENNIMAN and ROBERT BLACKWELL

Bright rock tempo

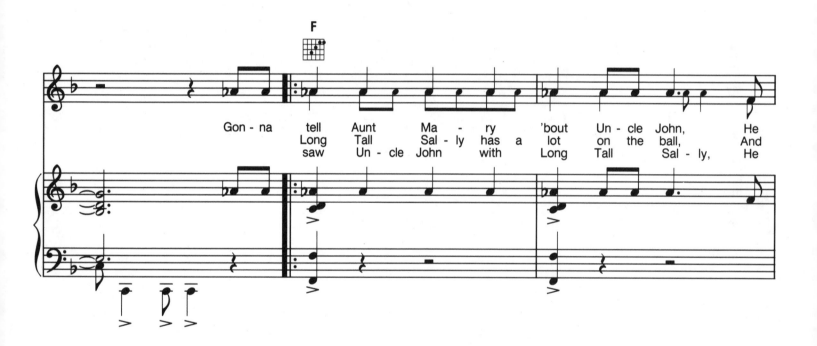

Gon - na tell Aunt Ma - ry 'bout Un - cle John, He
Long Tall Sal - ly has a lot on the ball, And
saw Un - cle John with Long Tall Sal - ly, He

says he has the blues, But he has a lot of fun, Oh,
no - bod - y cares if she's long and tall, Oh,
saw Aunt Ma - ry com - in' And he ducked back in the al - ley, Oh,

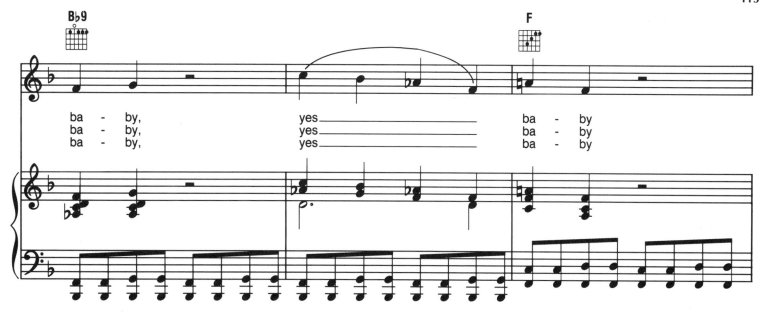

ba - by,      yes_____ ba - by
ba - by,      yes_____ ba - by
ba - by,      yes_____ ba - by

woo_____ ba - by,_____ Hav - in' me some fun   to -
woo_____ ba - by,_____ Hav - in' me some fun   to -
woo_____ ba - by,_____ Hav - in' me some fun   to -

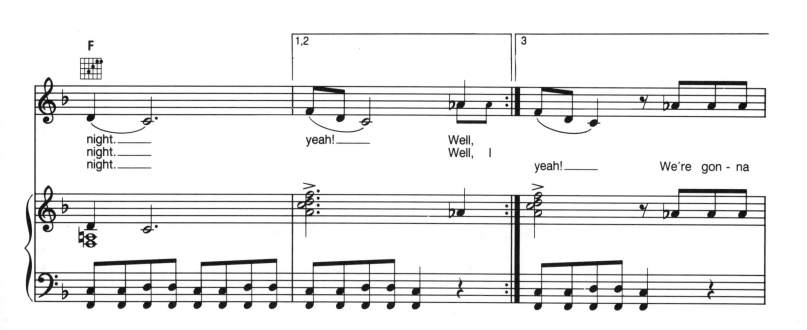

night._____      yeah!_____      Well,
night._____           Well,   I
night._____           yeah!_____ We're gon - na

# (You've Got)
# THE MAGIC TOUCH

Words and Music by
BUCK RAM

You've got the mag - ic touch, _____ it makes me glow so much; _____ it casts a spell, _____ it rings a bell, the mag - ic touch; _____ Oh, when I

# LOVE ME TENDER

Words and Music by ELVIS PRESLEY
and VERA MATSON

EXTRA VERSE   4. When at last my dreams come true,
Darling, this I know:
Happiness will follow you
Everywhere you go.

# MAYBE BABY

By NORMAN PETTY
and CHARLES HARDIN

Moderate Country beat

**E** **C#m** **E** **C#m**

May-be, ba-by, I'll have you.____ May-be ba-by, you'll be true.____

**E** **A** **B** **E** **A/E** **E** **B**

May-be, ba-by, I'll have you____ for me.____

**E** **C#m** **E** **C#m**

It's fun-ny, hon-ey; you don't care.____ You nev-er lis-ten to my prayer.____
*Instrumental*

# OH BOY!

Words and Music by SUNNY WEST,
BILL TILGHMAN and NORMAN PETTY

124

# MY PRAYER

Music by GEORGES BOULANGER
Lyric and Musical Adaptation by JIMMY KENNEDY

# OH! CAROL

Words and Music by HOWARD GREENFIELD
and NEIL SEDAKA

# ROCK AND ROLL IS HERE TO STAY

Words and Music by
DAVID WHITE

**Moderate Rock tempo**

Rock, Rock, Rock, oh, ba-by,

Rock, Rock, Rock, oh, ba-by, Rock, Rock,

Rock, oh, ba-by, Rock, Rock, Rock, oh, ba-by.

# PEGGY SUE

Words and Music by JERRY ALLISON,
NORMAN PETTY and BUDDY HOLLY

# PRIMROSE LANE

Words and Music by WAYNE SHANKLIN
and GEORGE CALLENDER

Moderate Rock

# ROCK AROUND THE CLOCK

By MAX C. FREEDMAN
and JIMMY DeKNIGHT

# SEARCHIN'

Words and Music by JERRY LEIBER
and MIKE STOLLER

Not too fast, with a strong afterbeat

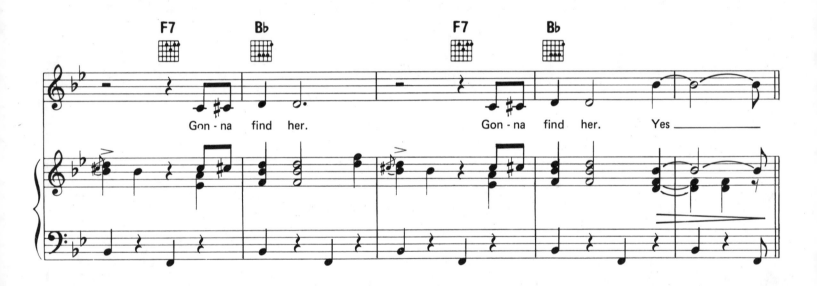

# SEE YOU LATER, ALLIGATOR

Words and Music by
ROBERT GUIDRY

# SHAKE, RATTLE AND ROLL

Words and Music by
CHARLES CALHOUN

Moderately Bright

VERSE

154

look so warm,— but your heart is cold— as ice. _____

D.S. 2nd ending

Verse 3

I'm like a one-eyed cat,— peep-in' in a sea-food store,—

I'm like a one-eyed cat,—

peep-in' in a sea-food store; — I can look at you,— tell you

don't love me no more.                    I be-

lieve you're do-in' me wrong__ and now I know, __          I be-

lieve you're do-in' me wrong__ and now I know; __          The

more I work, the fast-er my mon-ey goes. _____

# 77 SUNSET STRIP

**from the Television Series**

Words and Music by MACK DAVID
and JERRY LIVINGSTON

# SILHOUETTES

Words and Music by FRANK C. SLAY JR.
and BOB CREWE

# SIXTEEN CANDLES

Words and Music by LUTHER DIXON
and ALLYSON R. KHENT

# SMOKE GETS IN YOUR EYES

## from ROBERTA

Words by OTTO HARBACH
Music by JEROME KERN

# SPLISH SPLASH

Words and Music by BOBBY DARIN
and JEAN MURRAY

# (LET ME BE YOUR)
# TEDDY BEAR

Words and Music by KAL MANN
and BERNIE LOWE

**Medium Bright Rock**

**Chorus**

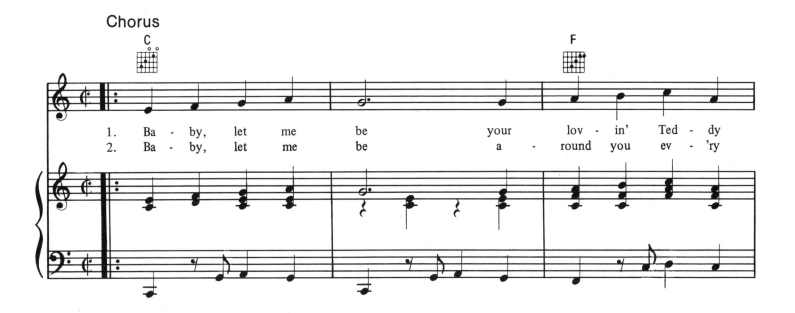

1. Ba - by, let me be your lov - in' Ted - dy
2. Ba - by, let me be a - round you ev - 'ry

Bear.   Put a chain a - round my neck ___ and
night.   Run your fin - gers round through my hair ___ and

lead me an - y - where.
cud - dle me real tight. } Oh let me be _____

your Ted - dy Bear. _____ I

don't want to be your ti - ger 'cause ti - gers play too rough. I

don't want to be your li - on 'cause li - ons ain't the kind you love e-

# THE STROLL

With a moderately strong rock beat

Words and Music by CLYDE OTIS
and NANCY LEE

# Tammy
## from TAMMY AND THE BACHELOR

Words and Music by RAY EVANS
and JAY LIVINGSTON

MCA music publishing

# TEQUILA

By CHUCK RIO

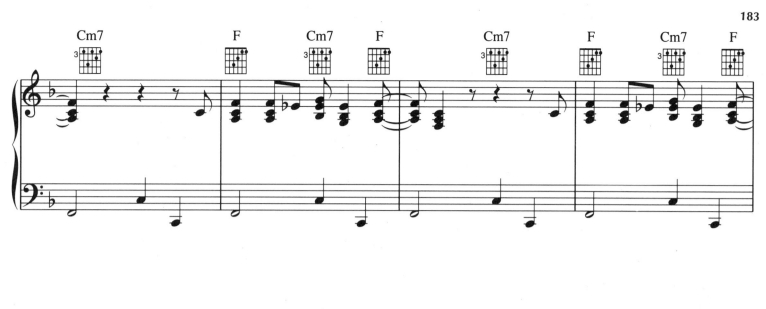

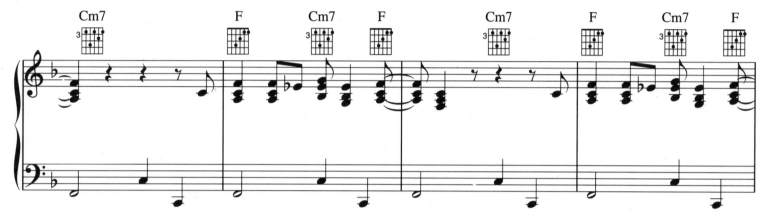

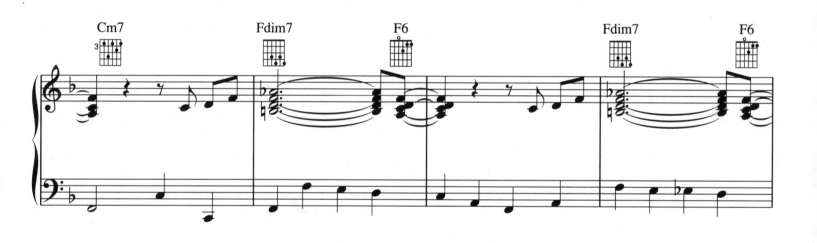

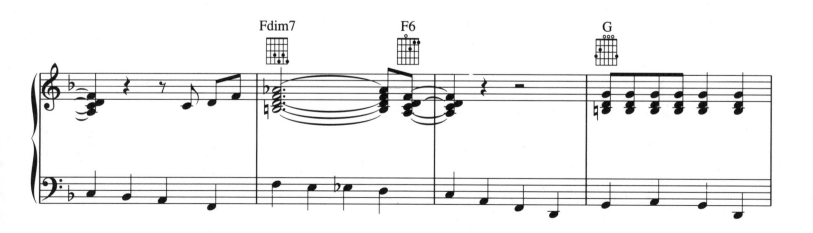

Spoken: Tequila!

Play 3 times

Spoken: Tequila!

# THINK IT OVER

By NORMAN PETTY
and BUDDY HOLLY

# THAT'LL BE THE DAY

Words and Music by JERRY ALLISON,
NORMAN PETTY and BUDDY HOLLY

Moderately with a Beat

Well, you give me all your lov-in' and your tur-tle-dov-in', All___ your hugs an' kiss-es an' your mon-ey too; Well,

you know you love me, ba-by, Un-til you tell me, may-be, that some day, well, I'll be through! Well,___

That-'ll Be The Day, when you say, good-bye, Yes,___ That-'ll Be The Day, when

# TUTTI FRUTTI

Words and Music by RICHARD PENNIMAN
and D. LA BOSTRIE

# VENUS

Words and Music by
EDWARD MARSHALL

# WAKE UP LITLE SUSIE

Words and Music by BOUDLEAUX BRYANT
and FELICE BRYANT

**Rock Tempo**

# THE WALK

Words and Music by
JIMMY McCRACKLIN

With a good beat

Verse

1. Well,— I — know you heard of the Su - sie Q,  And
(2. Well,— ) I — know you heard of the Tex - as Hop,  And
(3. Well,— ) I — know you heard of the old mam - bo,  And
(4. Now,— ) if you don't —— know what it's all a - bout, ——

Refrain

# WATERLOO

Words and Music by JOHN LOUDERMILK
and MARIJOHN WILKIN

# YAKETY YAK

Words and Music by JERRY LEIBER
and MIKE STOLLER

# THE DECADE SERIES

*The Decade Series explores the music of the 1890s to the 1980s through each era's major events and personalities. Each volume features text and photos and over 40 of the decade's top songs, showing how music has acted as a mirror or a catalyst for current events and trends. All books are arranged for piano, voice and guitar.*

## Songs Of The 1890's
55 songs, including: Asleep In The Deep • Hello! Ma Baby • Maple Leaf Rag • My Wild Irish Rose • 'O Sole Mio • The Sidewalks Of New York • Stars And Stripes Forever • Ta Ra Ra Boom De Ay • When You Were Sweet Sixteen • and more.
00311655 ...................................................$12.95

## Songs Of The 1900's – 1900-1909
57 favorites, including: By The Light Of The Silvery Moon • Fascination • Give My Regards To Broadway • Glow Worm • Meet Me In St. Louis • Take Me Out To The Ball Game • Yankee Doodle Boy • and more.
00311656 ...................................................$12.95

## Songs Of The 1910's
57 classics, including: After You've Gone • Ah! Sweet Mystery Of Life • Danny Boy • Let Me Call You Sweetheart • My Melancholy Baby • Oh, You Beautiful Doll • When Irish Eyes Are Smiling • You Made Me Love You (I Didn't Want To Do It) • and more.
00311657 ...................................................$12.95

## Songs Of The 20's
58 songs, featuring: Ain't Misbehavin' • April Showers • Baby Face • California Here I Come • Five Foot Two, Eyes Of Blue • I Can't Give You Anything But Love • Manhattan • Stardust • The Varsity Drag • Who's Sorry Now.
00361122 ...................................................$14.95

## Songs Of The 30's
61 songs, featuring: All Of Me • The Continental • I Can't Get Started • I'm Getting Sentimental Over You • In The Mood • The Lady Is A Tramp • Love Letters In The Sand • My Funny Valentine • Smoke Gets In Your Eyes • What A Diff'rence A Day Made.
00361123 ...................................................$14.95

## Songs Of The 40's
61 songs, featuring: God Bless The Child • How High The Moon • The Last Time I Saw Paris • Moonlight In Vermont • A Nightingale Sang In Berkeley Square • A String Of Pearls • Swinging On A Star • Tuxedo Junction • You'll Never Walk Alone.
00361124 ...................................................$14.95

## Songs Of The 50's
59 songs, featuring: Blue Suede Shoes • Blue Velvet • Here's That Rainy Day • Love Me Tender • Misty • Rock Around The Clock • Satin Doll • Tammy • Three Coins In The Fountain • Young At Heart.
00361125 ...................................................$14.95

## Songs Of The 60's
60 songs, featuring: By The Time I Get To Phoenix • California Dreamin' • Can't Help Falling In Love • Downtown • Green Green Grass Of Home • Happy Together • I Want To Hold Your Hand • Love Is Blue • More • Strangers In The Night.
00361126 ...................................................$14.95

## Songs Of The 70's
More than 45 songs including: Don't Cry For Me Argentina • Feelings • The First Time Ever I Saw Your Face • How Deep Is Your Love • Imagine • Let It Be • Me And Bobby McGee • Piano Man • Send In The Clowns • You Don't Bring Me Flowers • You Needed Me.
00361127 ...................................................$14.95

## Songs Of The 80's
Over 40 of this decade's biggest hits, including: Candle In The Wind • Don't Worry, Be Happy • Ebony And Ivory • Endless Love • Every Breath You Take • Flashdance...What A Feeling • Islands In The Stream • Kokomo • Memory • Sailing • Somewhere Out There • We Built This City • What's Love Got To Do With It • With Or Without You.
00490275 ...................................................$14.95

### MORE SONGS OF THE DECADE SERIES

Due to popular demand, we are pleased to present these new collections with even more great songs from the 1920s through 1980s. Each book features beautiful piano/vocal/guitar arrangements. Perfect for practicing musicians, educators, collectors, and music hobbyists.

## More Songs Of The 20's
Over 50 songs, including: Ain't We Got Fun? • Bill • Carolina In The Morning • Fascinating Rhythm • The Hawaiian Wedding Song • Malagueña • Nobody Knows You When You're Down And Out • Someone To Watch Over Me • Yes, Sir, That's My Baby • and more.
00311647 ...................................................$14.95

## More Songs of the 30's
Over 50 songs, including: All The Things You Are • A Fine Romance • In A Sentimental Mood • Just A Gigolo • Let's Call The Whole Thing Off • Mad Dogs And Englishmen • Stompin' At The Savoy • Stormy Weather • Thanks For The Memory • and more.
00311648 ...................................................$14.95

## More Songs Of The 40's
Over 60 songs, including: Bali Ha'i • Be Careful, It's My Heart • Five Guys Named Moe • The Last Time I Saw Paris • Old Devil Moon • San Antonio Rose • Some Enchanted Evening • Too Darn Hot • and more.
00311649 ...................................................$14.95

## More Songs Of The 50's
56 songs, including: Blueberry Hill • Chanson D'Amour • Charlie Brown • Do-Re-Mi • Hey, Good Lookin' • Hound Dog • I Could Have Danced All Night • Mack The Knife • Mona Lisa • My Favorite Things • (Let Me Be Your) Teddy Bear • That's Amore • and more.
00311650 ...................................................$14.95

FOR MORE INFORMATION, SEE YOUR LOCAL MUSIC DEALER, OR WRITE TO:

**HAL•LEONARD™ CORPORATION**
7777 W. BLUEMOUND RD. P.O. BOX 13819 MILWAUKEE, WI 53213

Prices, contents, and availability subject to change without notice
Some products may not be available outside the U.S.A.

## More Songs Of The 60's
66 songs, including: Alfie • Baby Elephant Walk • Bonanza • Born To Be Wild • Eleanor Rigby • Moon River • Raindrops Keep Fallin' On My Head • Seasons In The Sun • Sweet Caroline • Tell Laura I Love Her • What The World Needs Now • Wooly Bully • and more.
00311651 ...................................................$14.95

## More Songs Of The 70's
Over 50 songs, including: Afternoon Delight • All By Myself • American Pie • Billy, Don't Be A Hero • Happy Days • Honesty • I Shot The Sheriff • Maggie May • Maybe I'm Amazed • She Believes In Me • She's Always A Woman • Wishing You Were Here • and more.
00311652 ...................................................$14.95

## More Songs Of The 80's
43 songs, including: Addicted To Love • Call Me • Don't Know Much • Footloose • Girls Just Want To Have Fun • The Heat Is On • Karma Chameleon • Longer • Straight Up • Take My Breath Away • Tell Her About It • We're In This Love Together • and more.
00311653 ...................................................$14.95

### STILL MORE SONGS OF THE DECADE SERIES

What could be better than even *more* songs from your favorite decade! These books feature piano/vocal/guitar arrangements with no duplication with *earlier volumes*.

## Still More Songs Of The 30's
Over 50 songs including: April in Paris • Body And Soul • Heat Wave • It Don't Mean A Thing (If It Ain't Got That Swing) • and more.
00310027 ...................................................$14.95

## Still More Songs Of The 40's
Over 50 songs including: Any Place I Hang My Hat • Don't Get Around Much Anymore • If I Loved You • Sentimental Journey • and more.
00310028 ...................................................$14.95

## Still More Songs Of The 50's
Over 50 songs including: Autumn Leaves • Chantilly Lace • If I Were A Bell • Luck Be A Lady • The Man That Got Away • Venus • and more.
00310029 ...................................................$14.95

## Still More Songs Of The 60's
Over 50 more songs, including: Do You Know The Way To San Jose • Duke Of Earl • Hey Jude • I'm Henry VIII, I Am • Leader Of The Pack • (You Make Me Feel) Like A Natural Woman • What A Wonderful World • and more.
00311680 ...................................................$14.95

## Still More Songs Of The 70's
Over 60 hits, including: Cat's In The Cradle • Nadia's Theme • Philadelphia Freedom • The Way We Were • You've Got A Friend • and more.
00311683 ...................................................$14.95

0395